Dedication

This book is dedicated to the countless parents who have embarked on the journey of conceiving using a donor. I know the challenges you face, the disappointments, and the overwhelming joy when you hold your baby in your arms.

May *Our Perfect Chocolate Chip Cookie* give you the language you need to share this incredible story with your little one.

Special thanks to my partner, Anneline Breetzke, for bringing my story to life!

Mei and her mommies were in the kitchen baking when they started to tell her a story...

I ♥ U
B
A C
OATMEAL
MILK

Making you was like making
a chocolate chip cookie!

Your mommies had all the ingredients we needed but were missing the chocolate chips.

So we went to the chocolate chip factory

where there were hundreds of chocolate chips to choose from.

There was dark chocolate,
milk chocolate, white chocolate,

and even butterscotch chocolate chips to choose from.

Your mommies picked the perfect chocolate chips

and brought those chocolate chips home.

VANILLA
EXTRACT
We mixed them together with all
the other important ingredients:

love, hope, family, support...

Then we put it in the oven (mommy's belly)...

Set the timer...
And 9 months later, out popped you!

Our perfect chocolate chip cookie!

And you're lucky we haven't eaten you yet!

CHOCOLATE CHIPS
WATER

differences

1.Glass of milk on the counter 2.Cookie on the green board 3. Glasses on the stool 4. Blue plate on the shelf

Colour in your chocolate chip cookie

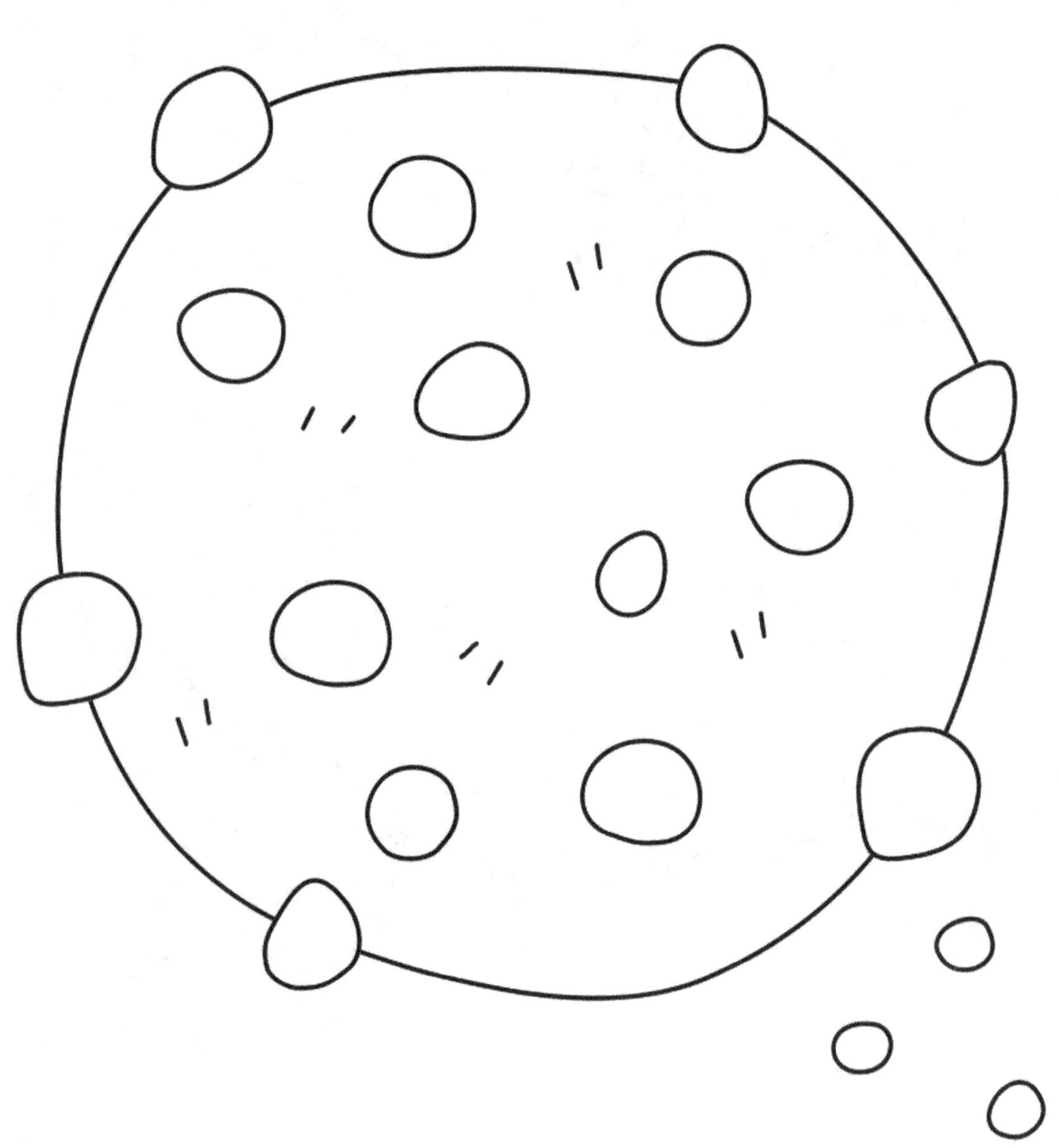

Colour in the family

Find the chocolate chip cookie

www.ingramcontent.com/pod-product-compliance
Lightning Source LLC
Chambersburg PA
CBHW080508030726
47592CB00011B/3294